William Bolcom

Mysteries

for Organ

Commissioned 1976
by Walter Holtkamp, Jr. for the
Hartt School of Music
Contemporary Organ Music Festival
Premiere performance by William Albright

ISBN 978-1-4803-9443-8

EDWARD B. MARKS MUSIC COMPANY | Exclusively Distributed By HAL•LEONARD® CORPORATION
7777 W. BLUEMOUND RD. P.O. BOX 13819 MILWAUKEE, WI 53213

www.ebmarks.com
www.halleonard.com

MYSTERIES
for Organ

1. The Endless Corridor

WILLIAM BOLCOM

Total Duration: *c.* 17'10''
(3'35''+2'40''+5'45''+5'10'')

Note to player:

Registration is largely left to the organist, except for a few suggestions here and there. The object is that this music should be equally effective on any type of organ, large or small, Romantic or Baroque - even on electronic organs. It is preferred that the four movements be played together as a set, for cumulative effect.

Accidentals retain force within beamed groups.

4

February 17, 1976
Ann Arbor.

2. Eternal Flight

Fast

sf   *sf*   *pp*

cresc.

pp

cresc.

pp

Broaden

1 manual independent of other lines, if possible

mf - *f*

f

f

f

Very broad

tutti cresc. - - - - - - - - - - - Full organ - - *fff*

ff - - - - - - - - - - - - *fff*

More movement little by little
legato to end of phrase

- - *ff* - -

Gradually close all Pedals to original settings (dim.)

February 29, 1976
Ann Arbor.

3. La lugubre gondola

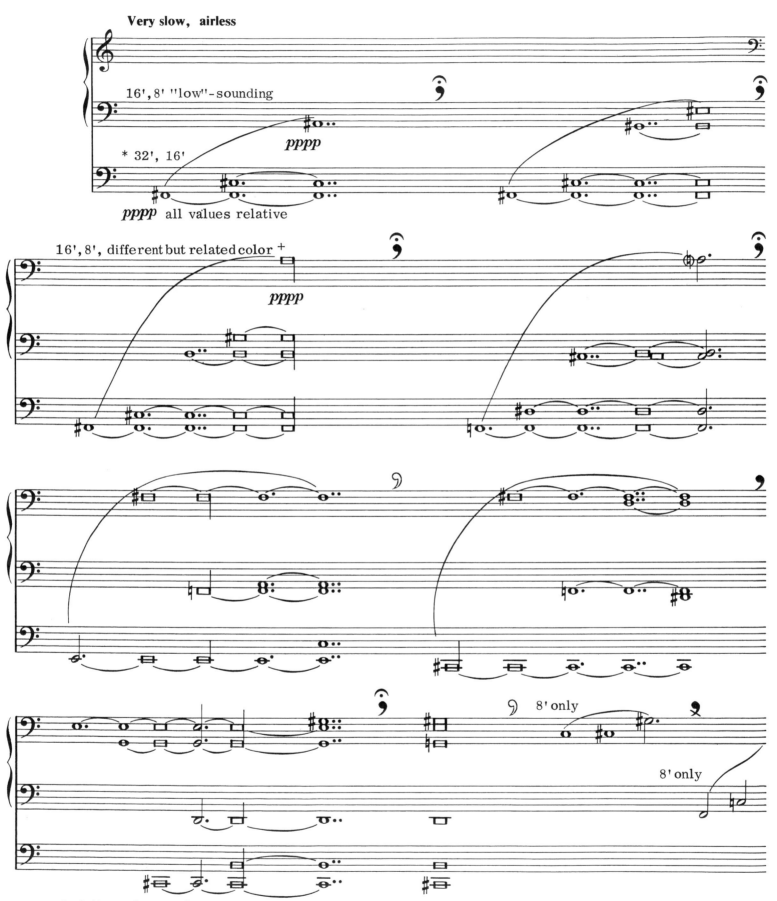

+a ◻ is 2 times longer then a ◻.
* If no 32' present, use 16', 8' for pedal, 8' for lower manual.

March 31, 1976, Ann Arbor.

4. Dying Star

Rather fast; quickly spinning figures (🎵 =140)

8' soft flute with much "chiff"

legato, even throughout

[32nds grouped for ease of reading only; accidentals apply within beamed (🎵) groups.]

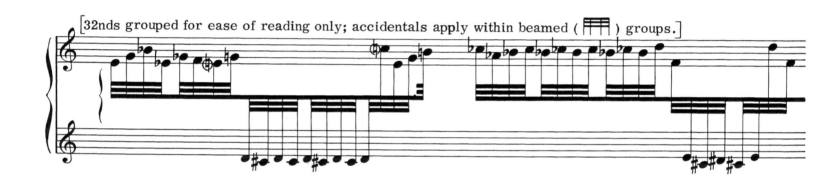

4' only

(*ppp*)   (enough softer to be subliminal)

(as before)

(*ppp*)

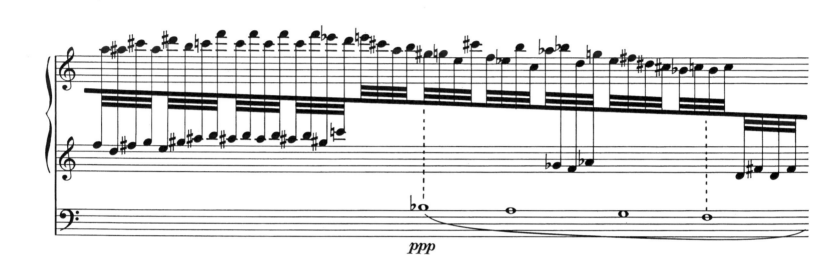

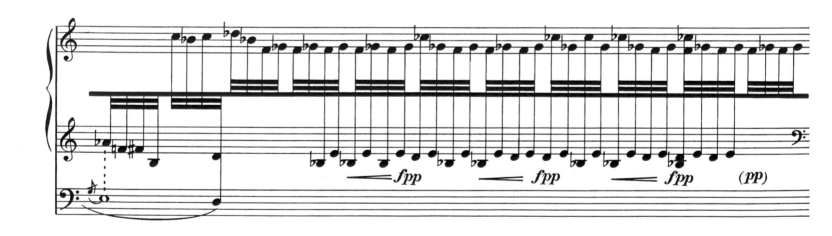

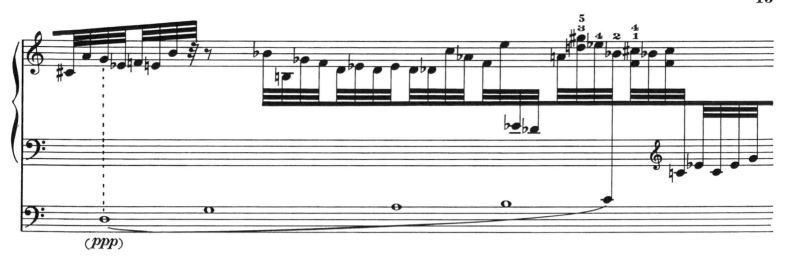

(*ppp*)

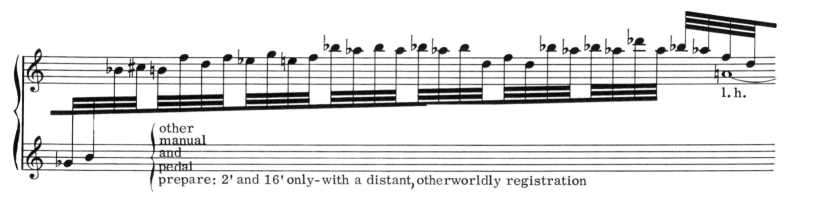

{ other
{ manual
{ and
{ pedal
{ prepare: 2' and 16' only-with a distant, otherworldly registration

l. h.

ppp   *pp*

("An Wasserflüssen Babylon"—J.S.Bach)

molto legato

as before

float in and out, like a radio
signal from a distant star

*These pauses are exactly timed - - be sure to remain physically suspended during them so that the tension is not lost.

April 9, 1976, Ann Arbor.